THE NEW WORLD

poems
by

George Evans

CURBSTONE PRESS

Printed in the U.S. on acid-free paper by Bang Printing

Cover design: Stone Graphics

Cover photograph: *Red Morning, Hanga Nui, Easter Island*, 2001,
by Michael Kenna.

This book was published with the support of the
Connecticut Commission on the Arts and donations
from many individuals. We are very grateful for this
support.

Library of Congress Cataloging-in-Publication Data

Evans, George, 1948-
　　The new world / by George Evans.— 1st ed.
　　　p. cm.
　　ISBN 1-880684-81-0
　　1. Vietnamese Conflict, 1961-1975—Poetry.　I. Title.
　　PS3555.V2165 N49 2001
　　811'.54—dc21

2001002309

published by
CURBSTONE PRESS　321 Jackson Street　Willimantic, CT 06226
　　phone: (860) 423-5110　　e-mail: info@curbstone.org
　　　　　　www.curbstone.org

ACKNOWLEDGMENTS

Parts of this work were previously published in the following:

"A Walk in the Garden of Heaven": The anthologies *The Other Side of Heaven* (Curbstone Press), and *Writing Between the Lines* (University of Massachusetts Press); the magazines *Durham University Journal* (England), *New Letters*, and *Printed Matter* (Japan); in Vietnam in the magazines *Người Đại Biểu Nhâ Dân* (*People's Deputy: Magazine of the National Assembly*, Hanoi), *Tuố Trẻ* (*Sunday Youth*, Ho Chi Minh City), and *Văn Nghệ Trẻ* (Hanoi); in the chapbook series *AIOU/le tourbillon suspendu* (France); on the web in English and Vietnamese at *Omely.com*.

From "Earth's Mirror": *Bongos of the Lord* (Japan), *Grand Street*, *Ploughshares*; on the web at *Salon.com*, and *KQED.com*.

From "Escaped Exotics": *Shearsman* (England).

"The Lightning Field": *Grand Street*.

From "The New World": *Exquisite Corpse*.

My gratitude to Wayne Karlin and Demetria Martínez for their steady light and kinship, and to these friends and readers: Claribel Alegría, Chris Appy, Jimmy Santiago Baca, Bill Barich, Gina Berriault, Kevin & Leslie Bowen, James Cobb, Cid Corman, Gloria Emerson, Martín Espada, Meghan Ferrill, Leonard Gardner, Matt Gonzalez, Gail Grant, Alice & David Halliday, Larry & Edie Heinemann, Ho Anh Thai, Ohnmar Thein Karlin, Christian Langworthy, Le Minh Khue, Kasi McMurray, Andrew Moss, Nguyen Qui Duc, Kim Stafford, Steve Vender, Eliot Weinberger, María José Zamora & Werner Ahlers, and Ofelia Solórzano de Zamora. Special thanks to Michael Kenna for the use of his photograph.

Amor de mis entrañas, viva muerte,
en vano espero tu palabra escrita
y pienso con la flor que se marchita
que si vivo sin mí, quiero perderte.

Federico García Lorca

for Daisy Zamora

CONTENTS

THE NEW WORLD

I

A WALK IN THE GARDEN OF HEAVEN

A WALK IN THE GARDEN OF HEAVEN

A Letter to Vietnam

1

They were talking when we entered the garden, two young people whispering with their hands, mist threads drifting from mountain tops on the raked gravel ocean. Islands afloat on the skin of infinity. The mind without its body.

"The moment I saw your face," he said, "was like walking into the Hall of A Thousand and One Bodhisattvas."

She had no idea what he meant, how it is to enter Sanjusangendo in Kyoto for even the fiftieth time and see row upon row of a thousand standing figures, carved, painted, and gold-leafed with a calm but stunned look of enlightenment, five hundred on each side of a larger, seated figure of their kind, miniature heads knotted to their scalps representing the fragments of a time when their heads exploded in dismay at the evil in this world, the way our heads exploded in the war, though we don't wear our histories where they can be seen.

Each statue has twenty pairs of arms to symbolize their actual 1,000 arms, these enlightened ones who choose to remain on earth and not end the cycle of death and rebirth some believe we go through until we get it right. They pause at the edge of nirvana to stay behind and help us all get through. It's easy to think they are foolish instead of holy.

Garden of Heaven refers to Tenshin-en, 天心園, the Japanese rock garden at the Museum of Fine Arts, Boston. I visited the garden with the North Vietnamese writers Ms. Lê Minh Khuê and Mr. Hữu Thỉnh, both of Hanoi and both combat veterans of the US-Vietnam War. They were visiting the US for the first time.

But each hand holds twenty-five worlds it saves, and because each figure can multiply into thirty-three different figures, imagine the thirty-three thousand worlds they hold, how much distress there really is, then multiply that by a thousand and one and think of what it's like to stand in an ancient wooden temple with all that sparkling compassion, even for those of us who believe in almost nothing.

It is said, and it's true, that if you search the thousand faces, you will find the face of someone lost from your life.

But the young girl in the garden was bored and looked over her lover's shoulder at a twist of flowers. Then so did he. The spell was broken.

We are older. There are so many wasted lives between us that only beauty makes sense. Yet we are like them. We are. They are the way it is between our countries. One talking, one looking away. Both talking, both looking away.

2

We entered the garden by chance. We were like the rocks there,
plucked from some other place to be translated by circumstance into
another tongue. In the silent crashing of stone waterfalls, and the
rising of inanimate objects into music, we remembered there was a
time we would have killed each other.

In the future we will think of it again. We might get drunk beneath a
great moon and see one another's eyes in a pool of water, or remember
in a glance across a Formica table in a kitchen filled with friends and
noisy children, or while walking down the street. But it will not be
the same.

It is called realizing you have lived, and it happens only once.

During Vietnam, which we say because the name signifies more than a place—it is an epoch, a paradigm, a memory, a mistake—during Vietnam, things were the same as they are now for those who are young and poor. We were standing around. There was no work, it was the beginning of our times as men, we were looking to prove ourselves, or looking for a way out. Some were patriots, and many were the sons of men who had gone to another war and come back admired. I don't remember any mercenaries. We were crossing thresholds, starting to lie to ourselves about things, and because we were there and ambitious or desperate, when they passed out weapons, we took them. We didn't understand the disordered nature of the universe, so disordered humans must try to arrange it, and if they get you young enough, you will help.

I'm grieved but not guilty. Sad but not ashamed.

That does not mean I lack compassion. It does not mean I sleep at night, or don't sweat at night. It does not mean it is easy to live.

In parts of my country, I'm considered insane.

4

Thinking of it in terms of your country, I could say I was the son of peasants. We earned or made everything we had. I learned to honor people for what they do, not for their positions. I've never been able to escape the rightness of that. To explain it in terms of my country, it means: if I didn't have enemies here, I would choose to live in exile.

5

We want the bones. We want all the bones. You will hear this. Good people will say it. They are all good people. They say it. They say: *We want the bones.* And they mean it, they mean what they say. They carry it into sleep, into their children, into the voting booth. *We want the bones. That's what we want. We don't want the ghosts. You keep the ghosts. We don't want them. Just the bones.*

Your ghosts are driving us out of our minds.

6

In my country we shift blame. After the war, those who went became
pariahs. Not the ones who started it, not the ones who carried it. And
because not everyone can overlook rejection or memory, more who
went have died by their own hand than by your mines or bullets.
There are more suicides among us now than names on our monument
in the capital, our broken dash against the landscape, scar that would
span the city if it listed the actual dead, black river that would surge
across the country if it listed everyone ruined on every side.

I want this remembering to end, yet cannot let it. It's like drinking the
ocean, but someone must remember, someone refuse to be tethered.

I visited your country at the wrong time, but if I had not I still would
not understand the nature of things, would still think my country is
paradise, which in many ways it is, but which it is not. It is built on
graves, on bones, on promises broken and nightmares kept, on graves
that howl deep in the earth, on skulls crushed with religious objects,
on human skin used as rugs, on graves upon graves of graves. And we
are always busy conquering ourselves.

Whatever it is holds us in a spell of wonder when we are children,
abandoned me when the war began. I don't mean just me or just
youth, I mean something about this country. But I don't mean just
this country, I mean the world. I've spent my time searching for what
it is, like a suicide who refuses to die, an optimist who is empty, a
buoy on the sea.

In the dry garden where we walked, where stone represents water as well as itself, the characters of its name meaning the center or heart of heaven (天 for heaven, 心 for center or heart), there is a mountain represented, Mount Sumeru, the highest peak of every world, every world a Bodhisattva holds in its hands, every world in the universe, and every world we live in, but it also represents the center of infinity, and because infinity has only centers, we were standing everywhere at once, and exchanged what could not be stated except in language which could never be spoken.

But we must speak it. The question is, how many heads do we have and how many arms and how many worlds do we hold, and just how far will we go to end our war.

8

The order of the universe is that there may be none, not like glasses lined up, each dish upon its shelf. And what we think is wild is not.

I want to be reasonable, it is something that interests, even haunts me, but given certain knowledge, how to be is more hellish.

The room here is small, and at times the way wind blows over the fence lip reminds me of animal howling and that in turn of an even smaller room, a box of sorts within a building stilted off the ground beneath a tin washboard roof hammered by rain in your country.

Our rooms there were perimeters not unlike the skin, and came to mean everything for each one, for each had the need to live in containment, to confine ourselves, as one might a crazed dog until it calms.

Perhaps it is not the past I should concern myself with, but not to speak of it and face what is still happening is not possible.

The double bonds of living for something and dying for something are ribbons that trail from us, drag behind or flap from us, and if I could understand it now or ever this business would be done.

I want to be reasonable, it is something I crave and wish I knew how to pray for but cannot pray, not having the faith of it, having seen.

We have friends, then we do not have them because we reach some border across which words cannot manage, across which silence will not bridge, and in the manner of children we stand without explanation or understanding, and there is no necessity that we question it. We learn to ignore those events which remove things in the way that we know of as "Before their time." It's another weapon we aim at our heads.

When we stood in the garden and looked at the stone bridges
connecting islands on the gravel ocean, I felt the war lift from us in
flames, inch by inch flowing into stone like a river on fire.

We ended something walking together, and started something.

I've read the war is over for you, but have never believed it. Victory is
no balm for loss. Any of us may celebrate a moment, but we live a
long time, and finality is not what we need, compassion is what we
need. Let the future think about the war being over, because then it
will be.

We can't afford to heal. If we do, we'll forget, and if we forget, it will
start again.

We've destroyed too much to be sentimental. We know that those
above and those below the jungle canopy killed anything that got in
the way, and we're all guilty of something. Wars are always lost.
Even if you win.

I returned to San Francisco sorry about some things I was unable to
explain, especially the army of beggars in our streets, and how badly
we treat the poor. The coldness of it, you see, is a symptom of killing
nations at a distance, or even up against their breaths. It has also to do
with how freedom can be like the end of a rope. It pollutes all notions
of beauty, this living in the streets. My wife in those days pointed out
that Americans do help one another during floods, earthquakes, and
conflagrations. "That's not compassion," I said, "it's convenience—
only generosity when there is no disaster counts." I'd become so wise,
righteous anger made me happy. We sat in silence after that.
Actually, one was washing dishes and one was peeling potatoes, we
could hear the rattle of a bottle gleaner digging through the recycle
bin on our sidewalk, a jet was passing over, John Lee Hooker was
singing on the radio, the neighbors were having a horrible fight, there
was a crash in the intersection, one of our cats spit at the other, and
the phone rang but we ignored it, so it wasn't really silent. Then she
said, "We would all be wealthy if people were born honest." So. Not
all understanding comes from the barrel of a gun.

Stretched flat in deep grass   resolute about the sickness of
pursuits   watching a moth on a beer can lip swing its curled
tongue like an elephant trunk across the water dots.   The only
thing I know about fame and success is that they are stumbling blocks
when they commandeer my attention.   My real function is to
think about things and listen, drunk and lazy, to the buzz in the grass,
the millions of insects who do not care what I think.   I'm tired of
the world of people—they're not to be trusted on the whole because
they don't understand death.   It's not that they're unhappy, it's
just that they don't understand death.   I'm not above or beneath
them, I'm just sometimes not one of them.   I've seen too much to
be fooled into thinking we know what we are doing.   Maybe I'm
getting too arrogant for my own good, but even that sounds stupid in
the face of death.   I understand the insects in the deep grass, even
if I can't repeat what they say.

12

I've come out to the cliffs above the Pacific Ocean before sunset. I told you my childhood friends were all killed in the war, and you told me similar things. It wasn't difficult for me to also tell you I was never angry at your country. What was difficult, was to tell you how angry I am at my own.

Pelicans overhead. The rose-colored hood of a finch in the bushes. I sit on a railroad tie post on a high cliff at the edge of North America.

Tourists drive up, take pictures, go home.

A cormorant. Sailboat. An Army gunship choppers over the beach.

Behind me, an Army base. In front of me, the sea.

I'm waiting for the sun to set, but it will not.

II

EARTH'S MIRROR

History

1

I sat for hours in a church and listened without religion or belief,
one without possessions worth a word, except this thread of
energy connected to the world, the gossamer on which I hang, a
man already dead.

Nothing I own has meaning. Only the touch of the living,
thoughts of the living, humans and everything living. Plus the
dead I've had no choice but to know.

The church was dark. A blindness seeded with murmurs, voices
of those who have plowed their innocence and planted things that
have grown against them. I wanted to say even the worst moment
saves us, even the worst thing we can't erase from memory is an
act against the time without time that's waiting.

Born to an era without mercy. We can't forgive ourselves, let
alone the world. A time when everything vatic is also vacant
because so many monsters have walked on the backs, on the ears,
on the foreheads, and fingers of those who believed them.

2

My sleeplessness betrays me.

All I ever wanted was to leave my tools at the end of the day and
come home.

When the work was meaningless, I ignored my judgment and
did it well. It was enough to sit on the front steps in early
evening and watch children play in that brief moment before
abandoning their dreams and the toys that mimic what is

waiting. There was something in their pleasure, their exhilaration at working brutally for free.

No matter what, I wanted my life to remain the same.

If I never left that neighborhood and the shadow of its factories squeezing a final energy from the evening sun, if I never fell in love with the crowd of faces and sweeping belief in others that drags us away (a child's notion that humans live on earth for each other), I wouldn't recognize this loneliness that eats me, or remain awake while I'm asleep, or be ashamed of my weakness, or know I became a boy who removed and devoured his heart with impossible love.

Light

Alone not in solitude but in a black sea
against night

where the swimmers too are dark,
and they are many, the onyx liquid dense with them,
black krill to be swallowed by a whale whose bones are black,
teeth and tongue and flesh and every molecule black.

They sink and rise against existence.
Relentless. Determined. Even in despair the arms the legs continue.

It's easy to forget there is a shore because there is no shore,

no advice will create one, no amount of struggle
do more than invent the mirage of one before it sinks in some horizon.

Love is earth's mirror, its deepest fire beneath the weight of oceans,
refracting the light of stars, the moon and sun,
the engine that drives us
though we are silly with the subject because times are bitter.

The question isn't how to know it, but how one could not know it,
not how to believe it, but how to disbelieve it.

There is no darkness, only illusion,
a creature, black breathed, splashed and racing in all directions,
a thing that caps the earth like the night sky sliding
from life to life, inching and heaving,
a moaning thing that rules, a tide
without substance that floods and wrings the color from human hair.

There are those it freezes into dreams, those it steeps
in fear, those lucky ones who die seeing it without thought,

and those who simply die without ever suspecting

that what they think is important are rocks mistaken for shore,
a coast it costs a life to crash upon.

Elisa Kneeling
(Tina Modotti, 1924)

This is the burned girl, this extreme photograph of one changed by disaster but unchanging. Her scarred hands the impetigo of fate. Her zebra hands. Her leper hands. Her scalded fingers. Her claws. Her face a chasm I wish to fall into, wanting moments (no, hours; no, days; no, months; no, infinity) in her hands, this one washed with blistering life, this scarred one, this face of everything.

The artist's servant, mesmerized with pain but ready to leap, kneeling on rock with a grief-stricken face, each morning she's up before dawn to sweep the house and make breakfast. How can the masters know they are served by a crippled goddess. How can they know her scars are from the same waves of a dark ocean that drenches them without leaving marks.

We are changed by this sea that engulfs us. Permanently, the way love's pain and beauty scars us and will not be removed. Stunned and altered before these eyes and hands, we could not survive beauty without its scars, that place we kneel on pointed stones, desperate for pain.

Soldier's Letter

So many months without word, I begin to wonder if I hallucinated
you, wanting confirmation that you too suffer, with no wish for you to
suffer. It's not easy to think of you in misery, but necessary. Cattle
are better off.

My world is tainted by what was innocent many lives ago, now
constant in harrowing force. Compelled to open unknown doors,
aching with exhaustion, it no longer matters how many dead I see; the
smallest mushroom is more important.

I've been to oceans, jungles, mountains and the desert, gathering
threads and twigs like a lost bird building fallow nests, each broken
branch the knot of a useless net, each inch of air a mile of sand to
swim. Where are you? Where are the words that poured a liquid
tongue into my ear those endless nights?

The faces here are unmoored, floating by disconnected from anything
but the unpredictable, even their bodies, like a field of heads bobbing
down a river, but ready to spring. I watch them with a third eye I've
developed, and imagine you in the farmlands hitching your socks,
tying your boots with a leg up on a stack of squawling cages, in a
kitchen chair or bath, your dress hiked crossing a field of flowers, or
naked with an ammo belt slashed across your chest.

When darkness erases everything, I fade into sleep that leaves me
awake until the squeal of pigs and migrant birds against the light that
keeps returning, days I relate to nothing but your absence, wanting
anything unfamiliar with the stench of gun oil.

Sometimes birds, what birds are left, land in silence on the stones near
my silence. Metaphors for nothing. They are birds, birds alone,
eating the air, the light, everything they desire. But you are different.
You stand for something. You may not wish it so, but even if you

abandon or betray me, your life can never again be yours alone—it has drifted into mine, where it moves with the force of a bullet.

So many months without word, I swallow desperation as if it's dirt. The world is collapsing around me, and while the crush of that is bearable, your silence is not. I must have hallucinated you. The one I embraced would never leave me alone, the arms that swept me through sweat and flesh would not have me settle for rifles and fear. The one I love would talk me through this death. You know how it is. We can't live for just ourselves, however much we know that trusting others is riddled with danger. But it would be selfish if I didn't trust you, or think of you constantly, sharing the same blood and being, the way mistletoe and oak share fluids, chemicals, the same end. It's just that I don't want to die without us tangled in each other's lives, without the weightless oblivion of one more word.

I know more than I wish to know. War is a condition, as if life is a disease. I'm being childish about your silence, childish because I know it's not your silence by choice, that you would never leave me without a word. Only, it's cold, then hot, then hotter, and I'm lonely.

I tell myself it's censors, slow mail, mislabeled envelopes, and do not want you to suffer, but pray that you bleed without wounds and gasp for air at these same desires, driven by anxiety, by memory of what glued our fingers together in trance.

I can't take my eyes off this possible last day on earth staring back from every angle, no more than I can take my thoughts from the eyes in your photo, which bears the weight of more than any object, any death I bend to lift.

Two Girls

That day I reached and swept the flies from the face of a Vietnamese girl on the bed of a pickup truck, until I realized she was dead and stopped, is the day I will never forget. Of all days, that is the day.

They crowded her eyes, until her eyes were as black and swirling and indecipherable as the eyes of Edvard Munch's *Madonna*.

When I backed off, the whirlpool revealed such beauty my spine melted. Such beauty I thought I couldn't live another moment. Such beauty my soul dissolved. My heart died and revived, died and revived, died and revived.

This pariah walks the streets remembering a girl. This one understands death's dimensions. This one dreams of a corpse without morbidity.

She comes to me in dreams, and at moments in the street after work, at five o'clock, in that ecstatic period before the fish markets close, and in my bed at night, where she still lives, as alive as the one who lies beside you.

Still Life

There you lie. Nothing a man of my qualities could ever say would track you down. I've spent too many days hustling food and shelter. My hands are scarred, and my face and voice, from hard labor and fist work. It was all boring, but all necessary.

By track you down I mean . . . I don't know what I mean. We search for many things at once. Right now, I'm searching for a way to talk a friend out of suicide during late-night phone calls, the static on the line an ocean between us, unable to come up with any reason that makes sense to him, except to say it's selfish, I want him in my life, and certainly there must be others, to which he says I'm self-indulgent. I'm also trying to understand ancient astronomical planetariums, the way a bird was glaring at me, something my doctor said (while the poor drop dead in the streets for lack of pills), trying to understand why a neighbor is pacing the street, a girl with a gun I saw, how the government gets away with it, a few words of Hopi, Maya glyphs, private armies afraid of the poor, the names of all trees, the birds and flowers, shrubs and rocks, the tribes, the weather signs, all the night sky that's visible through waste lighting, the stock market because it's connected to the real government, health insurance because it's connected to the real government, computers because they swerve and crash their promise into the same wall as somnambulist television, why the lights of a city across the bay glitter (it has to do with the flutter of pollution and heavy air), why everyone doesn't just shut off all the lights in the world for one night so we can all see the stars at once for once (it has to do with people sticking guns in your face, I know but don't care—we have all these guns because we can't see the sky and don't know where we are), and I'm harassed by people who just don't get it but won't shut up.

There you lie. Your arms perfect for battle and sleep. Eyes closed, watching something I'll never see. Relaxed as I can never relax. Your nipples hard for some reason. Even if you were purple, the morning light, which I have not slept waiting for, would make you gray. Your mouth open and volcanic. I will never track you down, but search with my ignorance, carry my puzzles as if they're profound, walk into rooms and look at things as if understanding their mysteries, wanting to, and will go on living as if I get it, going insane as many times as required, continue to die slowly, try to take you as you are, for what you are, for what you wish to be, impossible though it is to see through another's eye, or glimpse even traces of the true image of this other being cast before you in our common light.

The Comet

When it comes, after all the waiting in darkness over many days, over years and centuries, all who saw it last will be gone, as all who see it now will be.

When it dips and its tail flares a million miles of light, ask yourself how much pain is worth it, because when this comes again you will be nothing. Nothing you know will exist, nothing you felt, and no one you touched.

When you see its streak blurred like a spotlight in clouds against black infinity, hesitate, then pick up your guns and go on. Don't blame the moment for what might have been. What might have been is always at hand a crucial second before passing, in reach long enough to change course, then gone.

Love, not unlike comets, may come only once, yet how to know, how plan to see it, where to stand. In the comet's course, there's life then death then life again, and on, and on, sometimes taking centuries, which love does not. In these hard times it's not to show its face at all, go away we say, or fail to notice, a choice we have, but the comet, any comet, is without choice. And looks romantic.

There's nothing romantic about love. Romantic is a description of ways we treat one another, but love is the equal of death and life—everything ends, everything starts at its touch.

Six Memoirs

Saudade

So many ways to view the moon—
how many eyes on earth   how many animals
and plants leaning towards it   or fish peering through
the roof surrounding them   who carry
the moon on their scales as they break through   and all the birds
and you   so many countries away
could be on the moon   not under it
and it would be the same

Memory

Winter came in a moment.
I was distracted, battling my heart,
didn't realize how cold it was
until I cut my hand and someone
else noticed the blood.

Earth became a revolution
passing without me, leaving me behind,
but it didn't matter.

Infidelity

The smallest gesture
magnified, the touch of a lip on the ear,
an unexpected caress in the moon-floating night,
a lover's urge to move close after passion is spent
when one is accustomed only to silence,
little response, or none—
the stricken heart races
at just the shadow
of a whip

The Night Lover/Galán de noche

It comes on invisible waves
through streets and closed windows,
into deepest prisons with their stench and mangled spirits,
into rooms of deathwatch where everyone droops,
to the widower's bedroom of yellowing sheets and eyes,

flower releasing its fragrance at night,
blossom of the dark so strong
its aroma surrounds you
until certain of someone's presence
you reach to embrace,
grabbing the air, stunned by deception
you wish to repeat wish
never ended that moment
when doubts
caused by loss
overwhelm you

and the lover is gone
but the perfume remains

Avian Testament

I don't care about the news anymore—it's a product.
I've stopped flipping through papers completely.

I read, but to not read is like bleeding to death
without spilling blood.

Sometimes I smoke, sometimes
sit out in the sun with a beer
watching the local flock of parrots cross from their trees
down to the waterfront and back,
squabbling, flying
in what seems chaos because of the noise.

But if you look you see
they maintain specific distance
and closeness to one another.

I know each of them
and know

it depends on the time of day,
or on the day itself,
the way they fly that is,
and who they're next to
or avoiding.

They don't think about it much,
or waste time
worrying if they're wrong.

They just fly.

When you wrap your legs around me
the world ends.

By Full Moon

Bright as moonlight is,
Jupiter dominates the sky.

I watched it move southwest with Antares
by its side—scorpion's pulsing heart,
red/green double star that stands against war.

Alcatraz lighthouse flashing behind me
another moon.

When it lines up with the old prison,
the actual moon stands in the south
and Jupiter is gone,
though only to the eye
as you are

when I go at all hours
to watch the sky,
alone as any wandering star.

Under these smallest particles bearing light
(invisible ants of the universe),
beneath the canopy they carry to our eyes,
at certain moments I wish to live forever
and many times.

At first the gods gave me a hard life,
then they gave me you

and made it impossible.

III

ESCAPED EXOTICS

Walking Papers, I

Dawn beneath the underpass
        in rag and sweater heaps:
                mother asleep, urban
                        Madonna, millennial wool-sucker
                slung in a dishtowel
        against her chest, nipples
splayed beyond reach, dry

sacks, wooden pacifiers:
        citizen homunculus against
                her flesh, baby mouth
                        slack, arms curled, drifting in sleep,
                in motions of a death
        not death, tiny inhabitant
of invisible country.

        Across town, lovers embrace, as lovers must, glazed
        by muted light, bodies prepared to go on forever,
    as lovers' bodies will, stunned by the lightest touch, each glance
        transforming moments into years, as moments are
      on certain scales, all sound beyond the windows and walls
        laced with misery of pending separation, however brief
                the lovers' infinity.

Glow beneath the freeway:
    light of golden baby hair
            against near-blue flesh,
                the scabbed face of a young man
        dying of AIDS, his beauty
    obscured, friendships
perished among the mad,

impoverished, cut to shreds,
  a universe, a second moon,
    result of cosmic collision
      between two bodies—small one the rich,
    large one the poor, leaving
  behind a sphere that attracts
not sympathy but boredom,

  habitats lit by flashlight, streetlight, candle: humans less
 important than TV and the products beamed by its blinking—
  between those products the meaningless broadcast as news,
  weather reports from Mars, sports played by millionaires,
  police dramas showing how hard how important to control
  the poor, that compassion is best spent on those in charge:
  deep trance screen where sufferers cause the suffering.

Air rush, light flood, exhaust
  fume haze, sounds of money
    jumble in the money jungle
      mumbo jumbo finance scam: cardboard
    shelters twisting as they wake,
  blankets kicked to life—cocoons,
secrets, chrysalis nights, lesions

on the corporate brain—
  a million yawns in traffic,
    graffiti smeared on
      their concrete walls, shadows living
    beneath freeway troughs,
  existence as a nail in the eye,
lit match sizzling on its iris.

Millennial Flower Americanus

The child looks up with eyes
unlike other eyes, from the world
in his mother's lap,
cross-legged on the sidewalk
with her own eyes, bowl, sign.

He took a long time to bloom,
roots twining back to slime from which we crawled,
to the beginning, past Lascaux, past everything not a fossil,
and what he sees goes back through all
the plumbing of who exploited who,
which country won and what, which tribe,
which landlord started well but turned to scum.

History is meaningless to him,
whose eyes are rimmed with red, not from crying
but burning from the inside out, waking up
to this world, to now,
where simply being alive
is the only refuge.

Walking Papers, II

    Baby born in what dark fluids, screaming alley, car hulk,
border town, trailer hurtling north through the immigrant night;
  what flushing of after-birth down toilets, generations removed
      from sod eaves on the plains or wagons headed west;
      from what planet is it, this explosive wail and hunger
        muted then erased by stocks and bonds.

A sax wail rips
      from heat-blurred
          fire barrels circled
             by stamping feet and figures wheezing
         through rail and bus
      roar, morning stink—
what tribe is this,

           eyes opening
        in blanket holes to crash
       without moving, then voices:
        Get up scum
Police sticks rapping feet and ankles, jarring shopping carts.
        Up

One tries, falls back in trance, then worms out into oxide scent,
   the rusting tracks, a scene beyond a chain link fence,
       its corner warped for exit:
    two cars crushed, drivers throwing their heads
at each other between street people now awake, some crying
   some screaming, all fearing they'll be blamed.

The underpass city packs it in,
striking their cardboard homes, untying night,
those who live in shadows, on air, adrift:
their cups, tin cans, bits of cloth,
their wire and scraps of wood
pitied less than endangered whales or animals or land.

Their invisible country
of festering sores, flaking lips,
eyes that scumble the edges,
children who stare.

The Shopping Cart

A scorched baby doll with patent leather shoes painted on sits in the wire drop–down rack where children sit in the supermarket: one glass eye missing, a dented cheek, paper towel cape, dimpled smile, a turned-up nose, plastic yellow forelock on an otherwise bald head, its face looking up, head cocked in surprise, amphibian hands tied to the cart with baling wire. Next to it, on one side, a dented sauce pan stuffed with cafeteria salt and pepper shakers plus a plastic bread bag full of restaurant sugar, ketchup, mustard, mayonnaise, and relish packets. On the opposite side of the doll another bread bag, of partially eaten hamburgers and other fast food items, some in wrappers. Next to that, a half-gallon milk carton with its top punched in, filled with bottlecaps, a place mat woven from hundreds of folded cigarette packs tucked behind. Dangling from the frame on braided string pigtails that clatter when it hits rough ground: a bottle opener, a military P-38 C-Ration can opener, a knot of coat hangers bent in two, several panty hose fabric bags filled with discarded nails and screws, large loop of keys, a dashboard saint, tiny stuffed animal, pair of eyeglasses without lenses, and twenty-seven figurines of Mother Mary with hot pink nail-polished eyes, stuck together with Band-Aids like a cartiridge belt. On the front of the cart: a 5" X 5" newspaper photograph of a hand driving nails into a piano keyboard, stiffened by scotch-taped match-pack cardboard wrapped in Saran Wrap and stapled around the edges. On the cardboard-lined bottom of the cart:

cans of cat food tuna covered with a jumble of shirts weighted with firewood. On top of that, a layer of large and small plastic bags, an army blanket, scraps of blankets, newspapers, magazines, and a K-bar knife loosely wrapped in a camouflage poncho liner. Stuffed down one side of the cart, facing outward: a child's lunch box covered with Ninja Turtles and a decal of Mickey Mouse with a gigantic penis graffitied on—it is filled with plastic forks and knives, chopsticks in a rubber band, an ice pick, a church key, a potato peeler, an assortment of complimentary condoms. A broom sticks out from one corner like a mast, and saddled over the hull are pontoons of plastic bags filled with empty cans, strapped down with bungee cords, and under one of the cords a sign:

Walking Papers, III

This one, X, Sergeant X, ex-officio everything, vet and not vet
X, walks wrapped in his blanket through steam twist over
sewer lids listening: *Nicely dramatic, nice, nice, nice, like the
evening news*, one called Pinkeye shouts, *very nice, good
effect*. A loose one, strange one. Everything nice, everything
part of his stage, chanting *Pinkeye Pinkeye Pinkeye Poink*,
lifting foot to knee to perch.

Eye-in-the-blanket, X, slides up to the wreck, shifting in sleep
array, dishevel scratch—drivers take numbers, explain and
scream—he watches Pinkeye fidget, whose black hair is
twisted, sticking out like ginseng root, overcoat nappy with
fake rabbit trim, flamingo scarf, cherubic face, cynical eyes
with circles rubbed around the sockets, and who losing interest
struts the wreck:

Friends, subjects, and projects,
I'm recovering from everything
but god protects Emperors by driving them mad
it's a certain form of perfection
that is of course   if you know what   Medusa is all about
it's a question of looking the mortal in its eyes
haha   not just   haha   looking but

REALLY FUCKING LOOKING

at this nest of snakes   steady boys steady
staring until until until you're

STONE FUCKING STONE

unable to act upon E-E-E-E-E-Emotions

and but   *the tissues of love the tissues*
and but   **Pinkeye**   *the tissues of fate*
and but   **Pinkeye**   *coincide with the collapsing west*
and but   **Pinkeye**   *ern world and bring me*
and but   **Pinkeye**   *to conclude*
and but   **Poink!**   *everything should be as it is*
and but   **Pinkeye**   *in a Reynolds painting at least*
and but   **Pinkeye**   *with clouds like walls of cities*
and but   **Poink!**   *and sun like a living thing,*
and but   *delightful, delightful*

is the way it should be across my minions
and minions of minions,
my dears . . .

X hates these types. Too predictable.
Rubbing fingerless gloves together
he pays attention to what moves
in case it jumps.

Heat Wave

A flushed girl lifts her elbows and a man
        on the corner climbs out of his pants.
                A stretched-out tongue-limp dog
                        an island pumping up and down
                on the sidewalk moves for nothing.
        Ties loose, shoulder bags left on their own,
people shuck their shoes. Air-conditioning
        shudders and drips, air so hot sweat leaps
                off and sizzles on the subway grates.
                        Light poles and public phones
                untouchable. Coins leave a blister
        on your thumb. Paper curls and stiffens.
Matches ignite on their own.

                She sits in a bundle:
        wool cap, three shirts, blanket shawl, one glove,
        several skirts, knee socks, milk carton boots, scarf.

                Stares through the heat,
                through the crowd and buses and buildings,
                        right through the USA,
        across mountains, plains, cities, houses and gardens,
        cornfields, oil wells, nuke dumps, schools and farms,
            right through the middle of the whole hot tomato,
                        down the center,
                    the throat of the Capital,
        way off in some other land disconnected from people,
        some very cool other land of limousines and fine art,
                    world affairs and catered meals,

way off
where people
get their nails buffed and spines straightened for lunch
she stares,
not even caring
why everyone is crazy in the streets,
fanning themselves with their fingers,
wiping their heads,

stuck with their mouths wide open
like fish in the sun.

Walking Papers, IV

At times he is pure confusion, as drool upon the darkest drunk, beard streaked in vomit and mud, his heart a gnarl, twisted knot, record flung through space, who wanders off, who started pure, curious about even the air and where it leads, to come to this.

Another appears, screaming down the middle of Market Street kicking a bus:

> *I'm the shadow cast,*
> *dark swirl,*
> *purple blood rising*
> *around her bruised eyes,*
> *born into enemy arms . . .*
> *I'm not above the law, I am the law . . .*

wearing kneesocks on his arms with the toes cut off for sleeves, several hats, everything about him almost true but rootless, crazed but almost visible and exact.

Twenty years gone plus. Sergeant X. Traveling, humping heart-weight shifting to brain weight, his head many tons, who tried and failed everything, who walks with his head falling off, wished and shouted away, stinking of urine, evil, and insect blood: irritation, bat in the face, footprint on the face, snapped, unable to be willing to stay the same, too obvious, too gone, too nothing, too much, outside the realms of desire and demand.

Face as pavement.
                    Face as street.
                                        Blood as brake fluid.

                    Words as smog.

Creatures pierce and curl from his veins: false plantain flowers,
on worst days entire jungles, flower bulbs bulge his neck, his
fingernails serpent flesh, a thin layer of axle grease spread out
beneath his skin, his hair aching, inner eyeball a flame,
language a smear. Not that he doesn't belong, but that it's in
his head, the state of being non-being, common non-being, the
head and state of being common and non—end 20th Century
unto infinity. No more cowboys, no more unsettled west. A
blow-out among blow-outs along the road.

Drinking from memory.
                    Almost no memory.
                    Only war memory.

                    Now.

Earth Mama

Pushes her shopping cart downtown,
her bouncing baby holds to the wire,
up and down bounce,
upright in wind bounce,
whistling cart ribs combing the streets bounce,
picking the trash mama,
no dough no home mama,
homicidal mama,
hungry enough to eat baby mama,
welling grief and bouncing rattle mama,
pushing baby pushing mama,
baby's hands spread and knees
buckling as one learning to walk will buckle,
knots of paper cans and bones explode,
new population mama,
new class of people mama,
beat up, thrown out, raped and raped daily mama,
nobody's mama,
everybody's mama,
soon to be baby dead in a trash bin mama.

Walking Papers, V

The war is in his head today because of traffic crashing, because of smoke at dawn, because of baby wail echoes in the underpass and crevices in his white hands turned black, because he lives in the street and never gets home, because he dreams in Vietnamese and the top of his head is fringed by storms, because he's too specific and public about his pain and his lips detach and fly through fan blades, because his hands shake and he doesn't forget properly, because he was a soldier and junkie but can't remember which was worse, which ate his brain, which spit it out. Because starred nights pass over and through him in seconds, because days have no time structure and he looks crazy, because he is crazy, because he knows he's crazy and because everyone keeps saying he's crazy he's crazy.

The war is in his head today because it's cathartic, because that's where it belongs, because that's what he's about, because he held tiny white bones in his hands, because those bones were attached to a baby, because the baby looked at him and saw him, because half the baby was suddenly missing, because he was holding the baby but someone came up from behind and cut it, because he's still holding the baby, because he got a medal for holding the baby, because he hates himself for who came up behind to cut the baby in half which he was holding, because he was holding the baby, because he's still holding the baby, and because it is Wednesday.

Most definitely because it is Wednesday.

Victor of the Wolves

On Market Street, a tow truck jerks the wheelless van away where
Victor of the Wolves lives, one who gives everyone a colored wolf
name: Blue Wolf, Black Wolf, Purple Wolf, White Wolf, Gold Wolf,
Silver Wolf, Yellow Wolf, Red Wolf, explaining he's organizing teams
for a universal worldwide checker championship under the freeways
of America, and who named one guy Pinkeye, saying he'd run out of
wolf colors, besides which he didn't deserve to be a wolf because he
drooled in his sleep, and who stuck out his arm to a guy who looked
like a vet, naming him Green Wolf for the camouflage fatigues and
teeth, then shook his hand, *This is my promotion, mine*, he said, leaving
sticky marks upon the filthy palm.

Victor, sitting on a curb
　　　　　near the grease shadow of the van,
　　　　　belongings heaped beside him,
　　　head down, a thin line of drool upon his chin,
　　　　　　talking:

> *Dump the fuck they said,*
> *the fuck, the dump,*
> *I'm not a fuck dump,*
> *I'm a WOLF*

　　　Near him the black shadow,
　　　　　oil stain,
　　　mark of the van hull
　　　　where he lived,
　　　　plunging hole,
　often sealed and devoured
by the black vapor of sleep,
　　　the only country
　　　he felt safe

One wolf is standing on an updraft grate with his shirt open drying
from a bath in the fountain, another is stretched under a shaft of

sunlight pinning him to a concrete pier, and an old woman wolf, her several coats hung in a tree, slices the air with her arms and spins in a babble dance for Victor, who slides into a trance, on this clear day while a marching band goes by, leaving him doubled over like a country devastated by freedom.

Walking Papers, VI

He is walking around town thinking:

Their hearts were skinned fists, their hearts red mating calls. Their tears were sounds hitting tin, like biting eyes in their hearts on fire.

He is feeling:

My teeth are sawblades, fingers creatures, my brain is melting, vibrating legs, hunger, regret springs through my brain, my brain is melting, tongue spread flat pouring down my throat, a liquid tongue flowing backwards into stomach, kidney, bowel, the intestine pulled out through my ears and marched building to building, my brain is melting, scabs on my abdomen are moving, lice eating me as I am eating the air, as I am lice, as we are all.

El tren

He placed his head upon the rail,
put his head down
on the track, his
globe, his
lamp, his
bone-cage hell,
his tool, his past
and all known grace,
against the cold hard steel
he placed his head where he could
hear the east coast wheeling west

Walking Papers, VII

He is chanting:

Florid immense jungle pattern of leaves, mandala of god, tornado of
green life, orchid stands, roots twisting, sweating, veins leaving my
body weaving into jungle bone and tissue, coat of the planet, loam
and compost skin of earth burned in, branded on smell and sight, this
war, this jungle, this thing, mandala of god I carry, weight of life I
carry, and weightlessness of death, pull me to earth, cover me with
sprays of petal and green design for one more night, another life,
another night beneath freeway roar.

He is seeing:

Everywhere insect-skeletal choppers flying wild tearing left right
upside and down, leaping spark-spit dragons invading blood and
lungs, brain squalor, time rising, blood squeezing through pores,
secrets and things that happen in the dark under time, under distance,
under scream and rage and wonder, a blood slashed tattoo on his
brain, himself waking up covered with roaches, a smoking skull,
incinerated noise blowing out of ear holes, a headless armless best
friend squirting fluid in a jungle, people dragged by the ankles with
their shirts peeled to the nipples, babies like stiff black crabs on a
heap.

And he is running down the street pounding himself in the head to
make it stop.

Wedding Bells

In early evening,
at rest on a plastic garbage bag
on the sidewalk,
curled with his back to traffic,
fetal on his right side,
facing the wall of onyx tiles that frame the window of Victoria Pastry,
under the display of elaborate wedding cakes,
without shoes, his feet
black as the tiles but without the shine,
he is chattering over and over
shut up, shut up, shut up, shut up, shut up
to the hopeful tourist brides who stand above him
leaning slightly to admire
the triple and quadruple-tiered white castle
wedding cakes in the window
manned by tiny grooms in tuxedoes
and brides with delicate veils
who smile forever
onto Stockton Street.

Walking Papers, VIII

He is standing quiet.
The black Pacific wobbles under him,
arch of the Golden Gate a crescent moon,
another bridge on the water.

A fog bank masses out beyond fishing boats,
the unknown rising in a blur.

His blanket snapping,
he stands silent except for wind,
the sound of earth in its spinning,
its whirl through a cosmos nothing understands.

He stares at the shimmering water, islands of scales,
the lights upon those islands eyes, and they are watching.
The voyeurs of the moon and planets and stars
with the lights of all cities cupped in their curves,
washing ashore, passing by, melting,
rising, dropping, coming again,
forever

Miss America

Foghorns bellow. Air stitched by sirens this cold summer's end
is the screen she watches, and what she sees she owns,
uncombed, wild as anything,
asleep by her shopping cart in orange streetlamp blur,
paper flower wired to her hair.

It was different then, back then,
when everyone she saw and everyone that died she knew,
streaming the orchards with friends to catch the last bus to town,
the only one that day, Carny Day, the day she won
a giant pinwheel guessing the weight of a monkey strapped to a dog.

That night her mother made lemonade from the tree.
They sipped it watching fireworks.
There were siblings, uncles, aunts, cousins,
and her parents in the porch swing discussing money,
pointing out swirls against the starwork sky.

She had a teddy bear and doll,
then a bad marriage made her forget everything,
lose touch, lose track, and when the welfare checks got cut
it forced her out to the foghorn bellows and roaming men,
that ancient pinwheel spinning, fluttering in her head.

Walking Papers, IX

He thinks of the rivers of his youth, liquid fields that could not be
sown or crossed, circles on their surfaces not fish but eyes.

He thinks of star and moon seeded racing water, human figures
bobbing on its skin.

He thinks of stumbling onto skulls stacked by a highway, the white
coal of them, the rattle and shine.

He thinks of fifty dog tags on wire around the neck of once-a-man
nailed to a tree.

He thinks of what men do to one another, what men and women do to
one another, what women do to one another, and what will not stop
any of them: not their livings, their religions, nor their pain.

He thinks his heart is parched by a thirst for color, turns north and
heads away, over the bridge, to another city, different only, because
times are hard on the poor, in its weather and its name.

Thelonious of Market Street

His clothing canvas-stiff,
twisted gutter butt stuck to his lip, ringworm circles,
he kneels and leans above a concrete bench,
fingers spread and poised, hesitates,
looks up at the right corner of the universe
for the bee buzz pitch behind his ear,
index finger dot dot dots
the ocean breeze flowing in from the ferry docks,
then begins, fingers touching stone,
to play for electric dancing bears,
a nearby card table merchant's show.

Their cymbals clack, they ambulate in pointed hats.
Bouncing wide-eyed, he floats to somewhere holy in his head,
eyes glazed and chin way up where the music goes.

Somebody's lover once, a real hot sexed-up dude
who could bend a quarter with his smile.

Someone's daddy once,
someone's brother,
some other somebody once.

IV

THE LIGHTNING FIELD

THE LIGHTNING FIELD

The invisible is real
Walter De Maria

1

It blends with the desert until you are struck by sunlight sparking on the rods.

You look but can't see it against brilliant sky, though once in focus it won't stop being seen, like subtle truths we bargain with and struggle to ignore.

Then it appears to have grown from earth, the quills of a subterranean, the spines of a whole field as a cactus, a model of infinity the desert doesn't need, but one that embodies time and light in an essence native to the space, making it tolerable, though still a form of destruction, as much that is beauty is, and as all touched wildness must be.

As the sun moves, the rods move; their colors shift. At noon they become invisible, upright sun blending them into land and sky, their glistening bodies prominent as it sinks, dyeing them while it drags

---

The Lightning Field *(1974-77), by Walter De Maria, is a work of landscape art near Quemado, New Mexico in a remote desert basin ringed by distant mountains. It consists of 400 pointed, stainless steel poles (lightning rods) two inches in diameter, standing at an average height of 20 feet, 7.5 inches, adjusted to the terrain so that the poles are of equal height, so perfectly aligned that it is said a sheet of glass the size of the field could rest safely upon their tips without cracking. They are arranged in a grid with 16 rows of 25 poles stretching east to west, and 25 rows of 16 poles stretching north to south. They stand 225 feet apart (311 on the diagonal), with the total east-west dimension of the piece running exactly one mile, and the north-south distance just over a kilometer. A requirement for viewing the work is that one remain on the site for a minimum of twenty-four hours. Visitors are driven in, then picked up at the end of the stay. There is a cabin for sleeping, and a supply of food and water.*

away into dusk, clouds shifting in flamingo and purple folds. When it's gone, the rods turn white but begin to disappear again until the moon transforms them to silver rows that diminish in vanishing points, mystery lines in blackness illuminated by stars, the tips of other rods poking back from the dark.

2

Rocks are flying in far-off cities where men measure resolve with fire, their exchange of words reduced to weapons, free moments to exhaustion, free will to bread.

Lives absorbed in struggle, time parsed by argument and withered, children reamed and doused and orphaned.

South of here, a border crosses the desert, an invisible curtain dividing earth into landscape and scenery—the first a geography to survive, the second a possession to protect. A fence and barbed-wire intellect. A beginning and an end.

Along it, tribes surge north. They see no threat in their own eyes, no reason in their hands to be stopped, no logic in splitting sand into one world or a next. They see only motion and work and living.

Here in the north, hunger is questioned by those who have eaten, weather by those who are warm, shelter by those who are home. We are high above the south, where truth is a form of suicide. It becomes the same among us, but slowly. We are free to have ideas, but there are no bad ones, only horrible enactments.

One shuts the mind to so much it destroys the purpose of sleep, creating worlds without sleep, worlds where the body shudders into rest but does not rest because the mind does not shut by looking away.

Looking away is the same as looking, but more intense. The effort is greater, the after-image taking longer to dissolve. As in this field, where space confined by the rods stands out from the rest of the desert when you look away.

3

Outside, near the towns and cities, and in them, the desert is reduced
to sewage troughs, undulating rolls of sand and clay converted to
toilets by Rotarians and tract-house artists. Tertiary folds ruffling the
highway shoulder bridged by roads are graffiti taggers' heaven, hiding
places for drifted children near millennia to have sex, tempting death
or sheathed, afterward spray-painting their dissent, lonely wishes to
belong that pale to idiocy next to marks left by the ancients. But who
can blame them. They are sincere. And they are lost.

The hard part is knowing that the poor flood north across the border to
own what ruined them, and that being fixed on possessions peels the
soul and pounds one senseless, but history isn't written by the
conquered, nor direction set by those who have been stopped.

4

In late afternoon, a raven passed back and forth above the field, unable to perch on the pointed rods. Two friends and I stretched out and watched its shape against vaulted sky. Holding the air with the tip of a wing, it wheeled and crossed and recrossed.

Someone told me once that if the shadow of a passing bird (a hawk in particular, or a relative) touches your car while you're driving, your destinies will all connect, and in their nexus your life will be solved, the solutions revealed. It doesn't count if you swerve on the road after shadows—it has to be natural, the way driving through once-wilderness spewing fumes, crushing mice and rabbits, seems natural. We were driving through mountains into Eastern Washington when he said it. It was something he learned from a Nez Perce with whom he'd traveled the same road years before. Hawks were crossing in rapid succession scanning for road kill, and, we thought after he told the story, taunting us. But the birds were so numerous we knew we'd have to go out of our way to avoid being touched. Every few seconds red tails appeared above the windshield. We passed near a kestrel hung against the sky like a bird crucifix, brushed near the swoop of an osprey by water, and were rejected by sharp-shinned and Cooper's hawks, goshawks, bald and golden eagles, and a turkey vulture uninterested in our future. We crossed the mountains untouched. It reminded us that you cannot pursue your fate. Go where you are going; it will be there.

Opposite gravity, birds carry inexplicable forms, noises, objects, things we can never see, so why not fate I thought, on my back in the desert, and, in that world especially, why not a raven.

One by one we were swept by its shadow, and when I stood up it happened: I saw through a blue range of mountains one might reach by foot in several days, and beyond them viewed our destinies connected in death. It was a practical fate.

Our bodies dissolved into salt, leaking into spaces made by creosote root, mixing into dry lake cracks and ruts, alkaline, basalt, precious metals, waste, our dust mixed in with radioactive sand, scattering a million places, catching the wind, going on, and I saw clearly it's not only to live that one exists, and that being optimistic or pessimistic about any of it is foolish. Our purpose is to govern ourselves with one eye dreaming and one eye on the difficult balance at hand.

Afterwards, we sat on the back porch drinking whiskey. Lizards bobbed. Ants perfected their mounds.

The raven disappeared in a spot. I heard its wings chop the air for miles.

Watch the rods. Wait for lightning. Live.

5

Everything is selfish in the heart.

The emptiness one feels is the collapsing of time
from a seed that has sprouted the end of time,
a seed we have tended carelessly
with meticulous inattention.

Everything is generous in the heart.

The emptiness one feels is that same flower,
the heart, which is too fond of life to wish it gone,
but spends its days worried over what
has not yet happened.

Everything and nothing is in the heart.

I watch an ant carry its planet—the insect Atlas—
and if one thinks humans are not immense, think
of that one, the size of two poppy seeds, and what,
if it pays attention, despair might really mean.

6

In early evening weedstraw started blowing down gully and wash, tumbleweed skeletons spit out in bristled arcs, the wind splintered with memories swept up as it passed: the earth, its rocks, a flashing snake, and histories in stone: a row of figures with arms linked millennia away, feathered dreams on an outcrop: one whose head was fire, outlines of many hands in place of statements, and precise marks for the motion of seasons and stars.

As its power increased, the air was torn brown, the dips and swells of sand became bunkers at the edge of a dust-blurred village erased by ancient bombs. When it hit in force, swallowing all sound, elusive thirsts locked down in shelter and one would swear the world was empty.

Facing its force, I imagined the body of war: a head rushing from a ruined distance, its tail diminished in a brush of bitter calm. Back turned to it, I searched through its forward flow for the moment it hit and went on, as if abstract force has clear beginnings, as if it is possible to make sense of men and women and what they do.

I saw only the past being swept up in storm.

Still, the missing remain among us. The wind takes them, but also leaves them behind. They own nothing, yet remain. We can't see them, but we look, and would reach our hands into any fire to draw them back, knowing they are there.

Then we die. We become the missing, and the wind keeps blowing. The water we drink goes on, its molecules will pass through mouths in the future, just as water that rolled over dinosaur tongues is sipped in the capsules we shoot into space.

And in this field the wind will keep blowing, bearing the shapes of all bones.

7

On another day in the world, walking and careless for a moment, I
stopped in Washington Square to listen to students debate the causes
of war. They were shouting, screaming, but on the edge of a dance,
the sexual tension between them much more interesting than a subject
not worth words beyond chanting: money, money, money.

I thought: they'd be better off in bed together in any combination.
They should have been at the ocean with gallons of wine, drunk on
the speed of their bodies. Failing that, I wanted them to stop talking
and take over, march the streets and take the banks, take city hall, the
derricks of black blood, the military with its medals and weird suits.
Take it, I wanted to shout, it's yours. It gives me an unreachable itch,
I'm sick of it, sick of petty affairs that eat countries, sick of morning
papers ruining days, radio voices poisoning coffee, TV eating brains.
Take it, I thought. Take over. Anything would be better.

But I came to my senses. The students grew calm. One of them, a
runt, held his pinkie aloft while drinking an expensive bottle of water.
Another was whining. They were artfully dressed in black, polite, and
the subject was a television show, not war.

What things are really about is always another matter.

The lines between subjects, the borders, are not even gray, they're the
same as the ground they cross. And where they overlap is invisible
because the world is bored with its problems.

One begins to think that whether or not things might come to a sudden
end is not what bothers us; what bothers us is that things might never
end.

8

Then the wind was gone, and daylight. In the distance, lightning began to unfold elbow after elbow above mountains erased by dark.

We waited for its approach from thunder, imagining its veins ripping across the rods, waiting for the metal to attract and harness its mystery. That night it would not happen, but did not matter.

It's not just lightning but the place. Not the act alone, but its potential. The journey, not just the arrival. Not only the thrill, but the wait.

We are all waiting for something, and though not always ready, we are always waiting, dying second by second, revived in each tick by what there is to learn and the urge to learn it. Disappearing at night into shadows like the rods into new terrain.

9

At dawn, the sun broke over a scarp lip, illuminating
the ears of a jack rabbit, its red veins attenuated
for an instant before it disappeared in scrub.

A momentary understanding of life.
Getting it, only to watch it vanish.

How difficult to live with inequities
and contradictions wrought by humans,
but how necessary, and how stunning
because of them the momentary
things, the patterns of being,
the way beauty has
of turning up seconds
before it departs.

I did not intend to come here and think about war
or death or fate, or even time, but the desert
is opposite what we inhabit, its geography
frail, its stripped down body so obvious
it is clear in each second that life is
a brief matter worth every degree
of effort it is so at risk, worth
all pondering, and pain
when it comes
to that.

Along the highway and on the road in,
mormon teabushes glowed, winter fat
blurred into sage brush and snake weed,
white and golden dunes were clouds
behind heat devils, and such beauty
leads the mind to think not only of what
there is, but of what is gone, behind, over,

in the same way amputees feel missing limbs,
vestigial shadows with weight and motion—
the past is half the reason for beauty,
the other half being the future it bodes in promise.

I envy the ocotillo its flower flames,
and the stoop of the kestrel, smallest falcon,
creature that lives but a dozen years yet lives no less
than corrupted heads of state, and the cactus wren,
late sleeper, cooling its beak on the cholla, condensing
and reabsorbing its own liquids to go on, and woodrats
clumped beneath cholla, living for generations among the spines,
and the kangaroo rat with urine so dense it crystallizes hitting the air.

There is no waste in the undeveloped
parts of the desert, no unintended death,
no death by economics, no patriot death,
just simple death, an end to the effort,
an end to having lived by living.

I envy even the sand that was once awake in this place
where the heat is so intense the air so silent
you hear the blood in your veins, you
become the jack rabbit's ears, you
become the sun against rocks—
so thin, so deep a glaze.

10

The invisible is real.

But like an urchin test,
its simplicity is necessary,

not wanted.

V

THE NEW WORLD

Translations from the English

NEW WORLD ORDERS

- One does not work at a trade, one works at a fetish.

- Abstraction is loathed as specific. Vice versa.

- Everyone drives a truck. Consumerism the rule.

- Phone and license plate numbers same as social security numbers (issued at birth), or passport and Alien ID numbers (issued at airports and borders).

- Meaninglessness is meaningful, fears are confirmed and dismissed. Fear is mandatory. Everyone drives a truck.

- Last one out is a Monkey's Uncle. Monkey's Uncles are extinct but wear white collars or ties (never both) and drive trucks.

- Taxes determined according to need. Need determined according to taxes.

- Trucks are forbidden as religious symbols. Vice versa. Vice versa again.

- The State is everyone's Monkey's Uncle. Monkeys are extinct unless permitted. Trucks de rigueur.

- Trucks extinct, but everybody required to drive one wearing Monkey's Uncle suits. Ties preferred. Gloves encouraged. Choke chains optional unless required, preferred, or encouraged.

- Arm spikes de rigueur and tiny pierced earring radios required. Tongue tattoos favorable. Four stars for perfect silence. Radar tongue piercings extra points.

- Trucks are back in and everyone drives one with Monkey's Uncle door stickers.

- All monkeys in headphones and dark glasses.

- Fetishes out for the next six hours. Uncled Monkeys in.

- All monkeys to their places, ready for unclefication. Tattoos de rigueur.

- Monkeys out, fetishes back in, tattoos forbidden unless same as phone numbers.

- Monkey's Uncle door stickers altered to say: "We can't afford it but it's ours."

- Monkeys back in but must be confirmed Uncles and drive trucks with appropriate stickers. Monkey Business Forbidden.

- Stickers out, and monkeys back out too. Monkey see, monkey do.

- Everyone to their trucks. No door stickers.

- Trucks are fetishes and de rigueur, but no doors. And no monkeys.

- Absolute miracle-ism forthwith. Miracles de rigueur.

THE PARADE

Ten straight rows of two hundred thousand full dress soldiers with glass eyes, marching forward shoulder to shoulder.

Marching behind them, one row of two hundred thousand smirking pasta makers in white hats and aprons.

Marching behind them, two rows of two hundred thousand poets with checks in their hands, chosen for their taste in shoes and their ability to shut up or dance on cue.

Marching behind them, one row of two hundred thousand stuffed buffaloes on low mahogany pedestals with brass name-plates, pulled on travois by men in gray business suits wearing loincloths over their trousers.

Marching behind them, five rows of two hundred thousand cheering citizens in designer jeans wearing brilliant-white high-top tennis shoes, horse blinders, T-shirts and baseball caps bearing obscure symbols.

Marching behind them, twenty rows of two hundred thousand full dress soldiers with their eyes plucked out and blacked in with shoe polish, ears plugged, and the national flag flapping from the bayonets of their outstretched rifles.

Marching behind them, ten rows of two hundred thousand battery operated TV sets on wheels broadcasting a loop film of everyone's favorite newscaster wrapped in mummy tape, wearing dark glasses, and explaining the political situation in Pig Latin.

Marching behind them, one row of two hundred thousand somnambulist masturbating judges draped in black sheets wearing sandals, reciting the litany of culturalism codified in the elected government's latest white paper regarding its vision of a perfect society.

Marching behind them, twenty rows of two hundred thousand laborers whose heads were placed in square metal hoods for the first ten years of their lives, chanting proudly: "When we sleep we cannot roll because our heads are square."

Marching behind them, fifty rows of two hundred thousand mandatory-voting booths on wheels with two buttons, one X, one Y, both of which produce the word YES on an LED screen at the front of the booth.

Marching behind them, ten rows of two hundred thousand bloodless lumberjacks in sequined bib overalls, high on synthetic owl pellets and lugging penile chain saws with nothing left to saw.

Marching behind them, one row of two hundred thousand disembodied numerically tattooed heads of dissident artists, writers, and political activists skewered on thin stakes held high by kazoo playing marchers with five-pointed stars tattooed on their foreheads and First Place Art Medals pinned to the lapels of their uniforms.

Marching behind them, two rows of two hundred thousand marchers in surgical masks and caps carrying giant white placards with a black question mark painted on one side and a black equal sign painted on the other.

Marching behind them, fours rows of two hundred thousand tonsured marchers in exercise spandex, wearing dried toad jewelry and chicken bone eyeglasses, swinging brass chains attached to books sealed in clear epoxy resin.

Marching behind them, six rows of two hundred thousand bellboy-uniformed scribes holding laptop computers like peanut vendor trays, led by seeing eye dogs and wearing neck braces that hold their eyes to their screens while they update history according to a tiny speaker sewn on the epaulet of their right shoulders.

Marching behind them, an infinite number of two-hundred-thousand-member rows of X-eyed people separated by alternating rows of billboards depicting extinct cultures, extinct species and circus animals.

SLEEPLESS DREAM

At first it appeared to be a scene of self-manifested fear, a simple dream, but grew more complex over time, more detailed, settling into repeated scenery, events, characters who reappeared dream after dream, then even in waking states to others, those who were not dreaming.

It happened in a wide valley with village dotted slopes, a line of soldiers undulating forward through it, tired, sweating, towels on their necks like snakes, weighed down with weapons, marching, walking, balanced on sand, then mud, sloshing ankle deep then knee deep, moving ever-forward towards some unclear objective, obscured by mist sweeping the valley into a blur, suddenly clearing away like a tablecloth torn from a surface, leaving them in the same place but moving forward, everything about them jet black: their painted skin, their eyes, their uniforms. But their sweat was white.

We are stone, they said. They said it all together, chanting in frightening, sonorous harmony. Stone. This, they said, is what you face. You become your father's nightmare, your mother's pain, the past and future follow you in constant, unprogressing motion. You are dead and alive. Calm and out of your mind. Then you stiffen, then you are stone, but your skin begins to soften, you begin to move, a statue crackling to life, except for the root stone, the seed stone, which stays hard always, a second heart. We are coming, we are going, we are there, and we are here.

Then the troops stopped moving and stood frozen on a slight rise looking down and around at a radiating pattern of bodies in every direction, figures from history, tribes and armies jumbled together, interwoven in a dead, colorful mass: tomahawks, howitzers, pistols and feathers, clubs, crossbows, shields and beads and armor, sabers, machine guns, flintlocks, catapults and bazookas. Slowly they began to loosen, stretching, their blood forcing itself through their veins. Then they started marching again through sunlight down the valley, their sweat chalk white. The landscape of bodies moved with them like a rug upon which they floated. They all felt the same things, the same emotions, interconnected, a second nerve center and blood system connecting their flesh to flesh outside their flesh, and they acknowledged it with that disturbing harmony.

Through fire into fire, destruction into destruction. The worst fear, fear of no center, no central point, the last fear, a transformation of worst fears into fear itself, which has no fear, being fear, which has no home, no center.

We are one, they say. We will always be. But can water feel the water. Or fire fire. And when is a dream just a dream.

RESISTANCE

In the cities and towns, slower ones were separated out and spoken to in low humming voices with sparking wires held against their ears.

Those who were potentially dangerous, who were not revolting but whose silence was laden with possibilities of either rebellion or false docility, were given large sums of money to become involved in lengthy, complex business transactions from which they would never emerge.

Outright dissenters were shot.

Those who escaped were banished in absentia and perpetuum for avoiding their fate.

Near the end, all sense of humor had been eradicated, but it wasn't missed, it was considered irrelevant. The point was not that one should stop to enjoy life, but that one should keep moving in order to organize it so it might be enjoyed later. But because later might not come for centuries, blank-faced workers slid up and down ladders leaned against massive new structures with full knowledge that the construction would still be going on the day they died.

Kept in well-lit dormitories during the day, they had sex under the ladders at night, looking up between the rungs for any stars that managed to glimmer in the gas.

THE SHINDIG

When the weekly ceremony begins, their thousands of pointed hats tip slightly down, their gowns are dark and they walk in step through a rebuilt forest, up torchlit granite stairs to the ceremony yard, chanting in low voices: "What is not told does not exist."

It is known as The Dance of the Dunces.

As counterpoint, blindfolded dissenters kept alive for the purpose are chained to hundred-foot-long granite walls built against plastic pine and redwood trees. One by one their throats are slit as the dunces pass, but they are loaded onto helicopters and sent to hospitals for recycling by a wave of trauma surgeons mixed in the crowd.

Over the moans and chanting, beyond a panoply of stuffed owls and wildcats wired to the branches of the trees, can be seen the nimbus of the ten mile wide swath of land stretching along the southern border of what was once the United States, from what was once California to what was once Florida, granted to Disneyland under the agreement that they build a continuous theme park from sea to sea along the southern border.

It is know as Walt World, where everything has a pleasant ending.

In the ceremony yard, everyone gathers in concentric circles, then square brass plates are placed on the ground in front of them. On the plates are a series of dashes and dots representing Morse code translations of forbidden notions, false history, banned literature, banned art, and the names of hated and/or banished figures. Once the plates are distributed, the dance begins. Drums pound in Morse code on the high walls surrounding the yard, and the participants begin stomping the brass plates, left foot right foot left foot right, repeating "What is not told does not exist, What is not told does not exist," until the nimbus of Walt World blends into the brightening sky of dawn, at which point the plates are collected, locked in vaults built into the walls, and everyone goes home.

THE NEW RELIGIONS

There's the police, then there is you.

There's government, then there is life.

There's adulation of family, then there is fact.

There are the benefits of education and the reality of unemployment.

There's the straight and narrow, and there is survival.

There is swimming and drowning, dancing and falling down, singing and making a fool of yourself.

There is the clock and then there is actual time, historical records and history, books and language, music and sound.

Then there is death and having lived an actual life.

FINAL PAGES FROM THE DIARY OF ONE "DISAPPEARED"

Watching the flowing whip branches of willow stands, I remembered what, as a child, I was told the first time I saw one: They always lean towards water, even when none is visible, because it gives them stamina, shape and direction, and a man should always lean in the same manner towards truth.

Such subterranean forces do exist, like all-enclosing shells of fire beneath earth's crust, or webs of bone, and anywhere you dig you will hit them.

In my youth, the difficulties facing my parents and neighbors were rounded and kept at a distance by innocence and fascination. I remember opening the small claws of a grasshopper with a toothpick without harming it, having it sit on my wrist like a watch while shadows of a race riot embraced the factory walls like black flames, and I built trails of sugar for the ants so I could follow them past the reddened gutter where a man was stomped for stealing a bottle of wine, and once I carried a sparrow, stunned against a window pane, inside my shirt until it pulled itself out on its beak and flew over a knot of bodies outside a labor union hall.

Eventually I learned to pay attention, but also to look for times when things turn upward in morning light, causing the world to lean and pitch forward, slightly but certainly, in a positive direction, like that moment in music which always comes, that thought or person, that word which takes you and will not give or loosen, and when what is unspoken becomes a welcomed refrain, driving or pulling the troubles the difficulties away until you begin to see again from some lost vantage.

I've watched the streams and rivers and lovers locked together, dreaming in the trances caused by motion, hypnotized by infinite streams of water life, and examined flowers and trees down to their faintest colors until feeling their roots bulge from me, throb through my head into sun. I've watched the birds live in spite of things done to bring them down, the way they move against gravity, run their families and flocks without legislation, do not need us and do not care that we know. For me, that was enough. The ability to see was enough, and to feel the range of things against my skin, relieved to finally understand that not everything can be known, but that one can know enough.

Still, when I went to war I learned more than I would have chosen. The birds and insects, sciences and arts, philosophies, even harmless neighborhood gossip, were reduced to nothing, lost in the din and never considered. But the worst of it was not mine, nor was it important to any of the trained. The importance of the whole could only be seen in the eyes of everyone who was not a soldier and therefore always on the other side.

When it was done, the wartime, for days I stood alone watching the ocean, the foamed and iridescent crests of it under the moon, the fire of it beneath sunlight, among millions of lives thrown onto the sand where I could never be the same, or young again.

I have since met and lived among those who will not read carefully, cannot observe that the smallest weed and its flower will hold a hill in place, will not listen to what may be heard, and may be trusted only to survive. The great palm trees and whales fill reality before their eyes, but only fear fills their lives. Their eyes are no better than paintings, ears as deaf as seaweed folds in tide pools, and watching them, living among them, becoming one of them, I came to realize why humans grow old and die. It is not confined to science, but could be confined to the heart . . .

PARTIAL TRANSCRIPT OF STATEMENT MADE
BY CHAIRPERSON OF THE COUNCIL OF
SECONDARY SPEAKERS AFTER IT WAS
PROPOSED, SECONDED, AND ENACTED BY
CENTRAL GOVERNMENT, THAT THE UNITED
STATES RETURN TO MONARCHY AS A FORM
OF GOVERNMENT AND AS A SOLUTION TO
ITS DISSOLUTION—FOUND IN A MUD WALL
WHERE THE COUNCIL CONVENED BEFORE
MANY WERE IMPRISONED, EXECUTED, OR
BANISHED IN ABSENTIA

It would be simpler if one person, or an amalgam
adding up to
one person, ruled human activity, but that could only be
successful if there was only one person. It is diversity, the very
nature of nature, which creates the human horror. Corporate
ambitions are not abstract, they are the spine of the otherwise
spineless. One must stand upright. Failure to express this
ambition in any form for fear of critical rebuke comes from not
wanting things to be unpredictable. A combination of control,
safety, and predatory prophylaxis are the solution, but because
it was believed we lived in a near-perfect society, based on
good for all, which could not become much better, the society
collapsed. Three governmental realities—known as The
Tension Triangle of Specifics—existed but were not fully
observed at the time of the collapse:

- ■ Balance power on the fulcrums of total control.

- ■ Base every action on the assumption that it is safest
  to maintain an environment where it is possible to
  encourage all elements to agree upon all things.

■ Sanitize society of its radical and or unpredictable elements by execution, long prison terms, drug addictions, a false sense of empowerment, or large sums of money.

Incomplete use of this tripart power structure (mainly a fatal concentration on the second point) worked for a number of years, but was completely effective on only the most primitive levels, and subsequently provoked the great period of unrest among the intelligentsia and educated disenfranchised which we all know as Crying Time.

That is over. The triangle is in place, on as solid a footing as the triangular looking structures of old Egypt.

THE NEW ART

At the first exhibit after the Art Czar took over, in photographs
on the walls of THE MOST IMPORTANT MUSEUM, babies stared
white-lipped from hammocks with heads the size of classroom
globes. The artist was happy. The wealthy benefactors who
financed his trip were happy. So was the curator. So were
the patrons. None of whom had to peel those diapers away like
scabs. The Art Czar was drinking in a bar across the street.

And then, since the educated middle class complained and
whined all the time anyway about what they owned and the
state of the world that prevented them from owning more, but
had, from the government's point of view, very strange
compulsions to seek out macabre and bloody things, and to
actually masturbate at depictions of suffering and perversion
rather than quit what they were doing to help eradicate it, it
was decided, via consensus tallied on the screens of new
telephone instruments installed in every home with newly
diverted military money after the end of what was for some
reason called the Cold War (in which many people, animals,
and some civilizations were incinerated) that everything would
simply stop and start over.

The first billboards appeared during the next week:

OK   OK   OK   OK   OK   OK   OK   OK   OK

OK OK   OK OK   OK OK   OK OK   OKOKOK   O
OK OK   OK OK   OK OK   OK OK   OKOKOK   K
                                                      O
OK OK OK OK   OK OK OK OK OK   OKO   OKOK   K
OK OK OK OK   OK OK OK OK OK   KOK   OKOK   O
OK OK OK OK   OK OK OK OK OK   OKO   OKOK   K
                                      KOK

OK
OK OK OK
OK OK OK
OK OK OK
OK OK OK

OKOKOK   OK   OK
OK   OK   OKOK
OK   OK   OK OK
OKOKOK   OK   OK

OKOKOK OK   OK
OK   OK OK OK
OK   OK OKOK
OK   OK OK   OK
OKOKOK OK   OK

OOO

OKOKOKOKOKOKO
K K K O K K K K
O
O
O

OK

This was known as New Beginning, and the first dissenters, who were shot in the head to exemplify the seriousness of everyone's resolve, were dozens of teenagers rounded up in every City—when cities still had names—for spray painting the billboards, and especially for doing things with the Os in OK, which is now considered a religious symbol and is the name of every city, river, ocean, mountain, valley, and country on the planet, which is also named OK.

THE NEW WRITING

All writing will be considered speaking, and all speakers will be held accountable. Vice versa.

All criticism will be considered jealousy and sour grapes.

All decisions will be made by committee because the individual makes hasty judgments, tends towards hegemony, unregulated nepotism, and uncontrolled observation once a self-decision is made, and—once out of control—the individual begins to lobby abstractions.

Imperfections detectable by the presence of hysteria and speculative conclusions will be sanitized.

Language must be flat and unabrased by tropes and curlicues.

There will be no poetry but I-based (first person pronoun) confessionalism or automatonic obfuscationism. Rhyming is preferred, and except in the case of "it," all third person pronouns will be replaced with "he/she" or "she/he" depending on the requirements of rhythm, but all rhythm must be of the dum-dum dum-dum variety.

White males will not write/speak about being poor, enslaved, or oppressed, and will not address subject matter from what is known as the Pre-Columbian Era, except to admit responsibilities and express guilt. Exceptions will be made in the case of translations from other planets. In addition, white males will not use contractions or grind axes.

All others will confine themselves to subjects having to do with being poor, enslaved, oppressed, or address subject matter from the Pre–Columbian Era.

It's preferable that women write/speak of child bearing/raising and lipstick exclusively.

The names of institutions and committees shall not be taken in vain.

No pain. No humor. No screaming. No insults. No assumptions. No dream-like ruins painted over the surface like the skin of regret.

GEORGE EVANS has published three books of poetry in England, and the collection *Sudden Dreams* in the United States. He has been a recipient of writing fellowships from the National Endowment for the Arts, the California Arts Council, the Lannan Foundation, and a *Monbusho* fellowship from the Japanese government for the study of Japanese poetry. Founder and editor of the popular public arts project *Streetfare Journal,* displaying contemporary poetry and photography on buses in U.S. cities, he is also the editor of *Charles Olson & Cid Corman: Complete Correspondence.* He has published poetry and fiction in magazines throughout the U.S., and in Australia, England, France, Japan and Vietnam. He has also translated extensively from the work of Nicaraguan poet Daisy Zamora and Vietnamese poet Huu Thinh.

CURBSTONE PRESS, INC.

is a non-profit publishing house dedicated to literature that reflects a commitment to social change, with an emphasis on contemporary writing from Latino, Latin American and Vietnamese cultures. Curbstone presents writers who give voice to the unheard in a language that goes beyond denunciation to celebrate, honor and teach. Curbstone builds bridges between its writers and the public – from inner-city to rural areas, colleges to community centers, children to adults. Curbstone seeks out the highest aesthetic expression of the dedication to human rights and intercultural understanding: poetry, testimonies, novels, stories, and children's books.

This mission requires more than just producing books. It requires ensuring that as many people as possible learn about these books and read them. To achieve this, a large portion of Curbstone's schedule is dedicated to arranging tours and programs for its authors, working with public school and university teachers to enrich curricula, reaching out to underserved audiences by donating books and conducting readings and community programs, and promoting discussion in the media. It is only through these combined efforts that literature can truly make a difference.

Curbstone Press, like all non-profit presses, depends on the support of individuals, foundations, and government agencies to bring you, the reader, works of literary merit and social significance which might not find a place in profit-driven publishing channels, and to bring the authors and their books into communities across the country. Our sincere thanks to the many individuals, foundations, and government agencies who support this endeavor: J. Walton Bissell Foundation, Connecticut Commission on the Arts, Connecticut Humanities Council, Daphne Seybolt Culpeper Foundation, Fisher Foundation, Greater Hartford Arts Council, Hartford Courant Foundation, J. M. Kaplan Fund, Eric Mathieu King Fund, John D. and Catherine T. MacArthur Foundation, National Endowment for the Arts, Open Society Institute, Puffin Foundation, and the Woodrow Wilson National Fellowship Foundation.

Please help to support Curbstone's efforts to present the diverse voices and views that make our culture richer. Tax-deductible donations can be made by check or credit card to:
Curbstone Press, 321 Jackson Street, Willimantic, CT 06226
phone: (860) 423-5110   fax: (860) 423-9242
www.curbstone.org

IF YOU WOULD LIKE TO BE A MAJOR SPONSOR OF A
CURBSTONE BOOK, PLEASE CONTACT US.